Plutus by Aristophanes

Translated from the Greek.

The reality is that little is known of Aristophanes actual life but eleven of his forty plays survive intact and upon those rest his deserved reputation as the Father of Comedy or, The Prince of Ancient Comedy.

Accounts agree that he was born sometime between 456BC and 446 BC. Many cities claim the honor of his birthplace and the most probable story makes him the son of Philippus of Ægina, and therefore only an adopted citizen of Athens, a distinction which, at times could be cruel, though he was raised and educated in Athens.

His plays are said to recreate the life of ancient Athens more realistically than any other author could. Intellectually his powers of ridicule were feared by his influential contemporaries; Plato himself singled out Aristophanes' play The Clouds as a slander that contributed to the trial and condemning to death of Socrates and although other satirical playwrights had also caricatured the philosopher his carried the most weight.

His now lost play, The Babylonians, was denounced by the demagogue Cleon as a slander against the Athenian polis. Aristophanes seems to have taken this criticism to heart and thereafter caricatured Cleon mercilessly in his subsequent plays, especially The Knights.

His life and playwriting years were undoubtedly long though again accounts as to the year of his death vary quite widely. What can be certain is that his legacy of surviving plays is in effect both a treasured legacy but also in itself the only surviving texts of Ancient Greek comedy.

Index of Contents

INTRODUCTION

The 'Plutus' differs widely from all other works of its Author, and, it must be confessed, is the least interesting and diverting of them all. "In its absence of personal interests and personal satire," and its lack of strong comic incidents, "it approximates rather to a whimsical allegory than a comedy properly so called."

The plot is of the simplest. Chremylus, a poor but just man, accompanied by his body-servant Cario—the redeeming feature, by the by, of an otherwise dull play, the original type of the comic valet of the stage of all subsequent periods—consults the Delphic Oracle concerning his son, whether he ought not to be instructed in injustice and knavery and the other arts whereby worldly men acquire riches. By way of answer the god only tells him that he is to follow whomsoever he first meets upon leaving the temple, who proves to be a blind and ragged old man. But this turns out to be no other than Plutus himself, the god of riches, whom Zeus has robbed of his eyesight, so that he may be unable henceforth to distinguish between the just and the unjust. However, succoured by Chremylus and conducted by him to the Temple of Aesculapius, Plutus regains the use of his eyes. Whereupon all just men, including the god's benefactor, are made rich and prosperous, and the unjust reduced to indigence.

The play was, it seems, twice put upon the stage—first in 408 B.C., and again in a revised and reinforced edition, with allusions and innuendoes brought up to date, in 388 B.C., a few years before the Author's death. The text we possess—marred, however, by several considerable lacunae—is now generally allowed to be that of the piece as played at the later date, when it won the prize.

THE PERSONS
CHREMYLUS
CARIO, Servant of CHREMYLUS
PLUTUS, God of Riches.
BLEPSIDEMUS, friend of CHREMYLUS
WIFE OF CHREMYLUS
POVERTY
A JUST MAN
AN INFORMER, or Sycophant.
AN OLD WOMAN
A YOUTH
HERMES
A PRIEST OF ZEUS
CHORUS OF RUSTICS.

SCENE

In front of a farmhouse—a road leading up to it.

PLUTUS

CARIO
What an unhappy fate, great gods, to be the slave of a fool! A servant may give the best of advice, but if his master does not follow it, the poor slave must inevitably have his share in the disaster; for fortune does not allow him to dispose of his own body, it belongs to his master who has bought it. Alas! 'tis the way of the world. But the god, Apollo, whose oracles the Pythian priestess on her golden tripod makes known to us, deserves my censure, for 'tis assured he is a physician and a cunning diviner; and yet my master is leaving his temple infected with mere madness and insists on following a blind man. Is this not opposed to all good sense? 'Tis for us, who see clearly, to guide those who don't; whereas he clings to the trail of a blind fellow and compels me to do the same without answering my questions with ever a word. [To **CHREMYLUS**] Aye, master, unless you tell me why we are following this unknown fellow, I will not be silent, but I will worry and torment you, for you cannot beat me because of my sacred chaplet of laurel.

CHREMYLUS

No, but if you worry me I will take off your chaplet, and then you will only get a sounder thrashing.

CARIO

That's an old song! I am going to leave you no peace till you have told me who this man is; and if I ask it, 'tis entirely because of my interest in you.

CHREMYLUS

Well, be it so. I will reveal it to you as being the most faithful and the most rascally of all my servants. I honoured the gods and did what was right, and yet I was none the less poor and unfortunate.

CARIO

I know it but too well.

CHREMYLUS

Other amassed wealth—the sacrilegious, the demagogues, the informers,[1] indeed every sort of rascal.

[1] Literally sycophants i.e. denouncers of figs. The Senate, says Plutarch, in very early times had made a law forbidding the export of figs from Attica; those who were found breaking the edict were fined to the advantage of the sycophant ([Greek: phainein], to denounce, and [Greek: sukon], fig). Since the law was abused in order to accuse the innocent, the name sycophant was given to calumniators and to the too numerous class of informers at Athens who subsisted on the money their denunciations brought them.

CARIO

I believe you.

CHREMYLUS

Therefore I came to consult the oracle of the god, not on my own account, for my unfortunate life is nearing its end, but for my only son; I wanted to ask Apollo, if it was necessary for him to become a thorough knave and renounce his virtuous principles, since that seemed to me to be the only way to succeed in life.

CARIO

And with what responding tones did the sacred tripod resound?

CHREMYLUS

You shall know. The god ordered me in plain terms to follow the first man I should meet upon leaving the temple and to persuade him to accompany me home.

CARIO

And who was the first one you met?

CHREMYLUS

This blind man.

CARIO

And you are stupid enough not to understand the meaning of such an answer? Why, the god was advising you thereby, and that in the clearest possible way, to bring up your son according to the fashion of your country.

CHREMYLUS
What makes you think that?

CARIO
Is it not evident to the blind, that nowadays to do nothing that is right is the best way to get on?

CHREMYLUS
No, that is not the meaning of the oracle; there must be another, that is nobler. If this blind man would tell us who he is and why and with what object he has led us here, we should no doubt understand what our oracle really does mean.

CARIO [To **PLUTUS**]
Come, tell us at once who you are, or I give effect to my threat.

[He menaces him.]

And quick too, be quick, I say.

PLUTUS
I'll thrash you.

CARIO [To **CHREMYLUS**]
Ha! is it thus he tells us his name?

CHREMYLUS
'Tis to you and not to me that he replies thus; your mode of questioning him was ill-advised. [To **PLUTUS**] Come, friend, if you care to oblige an honest man, answer me.

PLUTUS
I'll knock you down.

CARIO
Ah! what a pleasant fellow and what a delightful prophecy the god has given you!

CHREMYLUS
By Demeter, you'll have no reason to laugh presently.

CARIO
If you don't speak, you wretch, I will surely do you an ill turn.

PLUTUS
Friends, take yourselves off and leave me.

CHREMYLUS
That we very certainly shan't.

CARIO

This, master, is the best thing to do. I'll undertake to secure him the most frightful death; I will lead him to the verge of a precipice and then leave him there, so that he'll break his neck when he pitches over.

CHREMYLUS
Well then, I leave him to you, and do the thing quickly.

PLUTUS
Oh, no! Have mercy!

CHREMYLUS
Will you speak then?

PLUTUS
But if you learn who I am, I know well that you will ill-use me and will not let me go again.

CHREMYLUS
I call the gods to witness that you have naught to fear if you will only speak.

PLUTUS
Well then, first unhand me.

CHREMYLUS
There! we set you free.

PLUTUS
Listen then, since I must reveal what I had intended to keep a secret. I am Plutus. [1]

[1] *Plutus, the god of riches, was included amongst the infernal deities, because riches are extracted from the earth's bosom, which is their dwelling-place. According to Hesiod, he was the son of Demeter; agriculture is in truth the most solid foundation of wealth. He was generally represented as an old blind man, halting in gait and winged, coming with slow steps but going away on a rapid flight and carrying a purse in his hand. At Athens the statue of Peace bore Plutus represented as still a child on her bosom as a symbol of the wealth that peace brings.*

CHREMYLUS
Oh! you wretched rascal! You Plutus all the while, and you never said so!

CARIO
You, Plutus, and in this piteous guise!

CHREMYLUS
Oh, Phoebus Apollo! oh, ye gods of heaven and hell! Oh, Zeus! is it really and truly as you say?

PLUTUS
Aye.

CHREMYLUS
Plutus' very own self?

PLUTUS

His own very self and none other.

CHREMYLUS
But tell me, whence come you to be so squalid?

PLUTUS
I have just left Patrocles' house, who has not had a bath since his birth.

CHREMYLUS
But your infirmity; how did that happen? Tell me.

PLUTUS
Zeus inflicted it on me, because of his jealousy of mankind. When I was young, I threatened him that I would only go to the just, the wise, the men of ordered life; to prevent my distinguishing these, he struck me with blindness! so much does he envy the good!

CHREMYLUS
And yet, 'tis only the upright and just who honour him.

PLUTUS
Quite true.

CHREMYLUS
Therefore, if ever you recovered your sight, you would shun the wicked?

PLUTUS
Undoubtedly.

CHREMYLUS
You would visit the good?

PLUTUS
Assuredly. It is a very long time since I saw them.

CHREMYLUS
That's not astonishing. I, who see clearly, don't see a single one.

PLUTUS
Now let me leave you, for I have told you everything.

CHREMYLUS
No, certainly not! we shall fasten ourselves on to you faster than ever.

PLUTUS
Did I not tell you, you were going to plague me?

CHREMYLUS
Oh! I adjure you, believe what I say and don't leave me; for you will seek in vain for a more honest man than myself.

CARIO

There is only one man more worthy; and that is I.

PLUTUS
All talk like this, but as soon as they secure my favours and grow rich, their wickedness knows no bounds.

CHREMYLUS
And yet all men are not wicked.

PLUTUS
All. There's no exception.

CARIO
You shall pay for that opinion.

CHREMYLUS
Listen to what happiness there is in store for you, if you but stay with us. I have hope; aye, I have good hope with the god's help to deliver you from that blindness, in fact to restore your sight.

PLUTUS
Oh! do nothing of the kind, for I don't wish to recover it.

CHREMYLUS
What's that you say?

CARIO
This fellow hugs his own misery.

PLUTUS
If you were mad enough to cure me, and Zeus heard of it, he would overwhelm me with his anger.

CHREMYLUS
And is he not doing this now by leaving you to grope your wandering way?

PLUTUS
I don't know; but I'm horribly afraid of him.

CHREMYLUS
Indeed? Ah! you are the biggest poltroon of all the gods! Why, Zeus with his throne and his lightnings would not be worth an obolus if you recovered your sight, were it but for a few instants.

PLUTUS
Impious man, don't talk like that.

CHREMYLUS
Fear nothing! I will prove to you that you are far more powerful and mightier than he.

PLUTUS
I mightier than he?

CHREMYLUS

Aye, by heaven! For instance, what is the origin of the power that Zeus wields over the other gods?

CARIO
'Tis money; he has so much of it.

CHREMYLUS
And who gives it to him?

CARIO [Pointing to **PLUTUS**]
This fellow.

CHREMYLUS
If sacrifices are offered to him, is not Plutus their cause?

CARIO
Undoubtedly, for 'tis wealth that all demand and clamour most loudly for.

CHREMYLUS
Thus 'tis Plutus who is the fount of all the honours rendered to Zeus, whose worship he can wither up at the root, if it so please him.

PLUTUS
And how so?

CHREMYLUS
Not an ox, nor a cake, nor indeed anything at all could be offered, if you did not wish it.

PLUTUS
Why?

CHREMYLUS
Why? but what means are there to buy anything if you are not there to give the money? Hence if Zeus should cause you any trouble, you will destroy his power without other help.

PLUTUS
So 'tis because of me that sacrifices are offered to him?

CHREMYLUS
Most assuredly. Whatever is dazzling, beautiful or charming in the eyes of mankind, comes from you. Does not everything depend on wealth?

CARIO
I myself was bought for a few coins; if I'm a slave, 'tis only because I was not rich.

CHREMYLUS
And what of the Corinthian courtesans? If a poor man offers them proposals, they do not listen; but if it be a rich one, instantly they offer their buttocks for his pleasure.

CARIO
'Tis the same with the lads; they care not for love, to them money means everything.

CHREMYLUS
You speak of those who accept all comers; yet some of them are honest, and 'tis not money they ask of their patrons.

CARIO
What then?

CHREMYLUS
A fine horse, a pack of hounds.

CARIO
Aye, they would blush to ask for money and cleverly disguise their shame.

CHREMYLUS
'Tis in you that every art, all human inventions, have had their origin; 'tis through you that one man sits cutting leather in his shop.

CARIO
That another fashions iron or wood.

CHREMYLUS
That yet another chases the gold he has received from you.

CARIO
That one is a fuller.

CHREMYLUS
That t'other washes wool.

CARIO
That this one is a tanner.

CHREMYLUS
And that other sells onions.

CARIO
And if the adulterer, caught red-handed, is depilated 'tis on account of you.

PLUTUS
Oh! great gods! I knew naught of all this!

CARIO
Is it not he who lends the Great King all his pride?

CHREMYLUS
Is it not he who draws the citizens to the Assembly? [1]

[1] In order to receive the triobolus, the fee for attendance.

CARIO
And tell me, is it not you who equip the triremes? [2]

CHREMYLUS
And who feed our mercenaries at Corinth? [3]

[3] Athens had formed an alliance with Corinth and Thebes against Sparta in 393 B.C., a little before the production of the 'Plutus.' Corinth, not feeling itself strong enough to resist the attacks of the Spartans unaided, had demanded the help of an Athenian garrison, and hence Athens maintained some few thousand mercenaries there.

CARIO
Are not you the cause of Pamphilus' sufferings?

CHREMYLUS
And of the needle-seller's with Pamphilus?

CARIO
Is it not because of you that Agyrrhius lets wind so loudly?

CHREMYLUS
And that Philepsius rolls off his fables?

CARIO
That troops are sent to succour the Egyptians?

CHREMYLUS
And that Laïs is kept by Philonides?

CARIO
That the tower of Timotheus...

CHREMYLUS [To **CARIO**]
May it fall upon your head!
[To **PLUTUS**] In short, Plutus, 'tis through you that everything is done; be it known to you that you are the sole cause both of good and evil.

CARIO
In war, 'tis the flag under which you serve that victory favours.

PLUTUS
What! I can do so many things by myself and unaided?

CHREMYLUS
And many others besides; wherefore men are never tired of your gifts. They get weary of all else,—of love ...

CARIO
Of bread.

CHREMYLUS

Of music.

CARIO
Of sweetmeats.

CHREMYLUS
Of honours.

CARIO
Of cakes.

CHREMYLUS
Of battles.

CARIO
Of figs.

CHREMYLUS
Of ambition.

CARIO
Of gruel.

CHREMYLUS
Of military advancement.

CARIO
Of lentils.

CHREMYLUS
But of you they never tire. Has a man got thirteen talents, he has all the greater ardour to possess sixteen; is that wish achieved, he will want forty or will complain that he knows not how to make the two ends meet.

PLUTUS
All this, methinks, is very true; there is but one point that makes me feel a bit uneasy.

CHREMYLUS
And that is?

PLUTUS
How could I use this power, which you say I have?

CHREMYLUS
Ah! they were quite right who said, there's nothing more timorous than Plutus.

PLUTUS
No, no; it was a thief who calumniated me. Having broken into a house, he found everything locked up and could take nothing, so he dubbed my prudence fear.

CHREMYLUS

Don't be disturbed; if you support me zealously, I'll make you more sharp-sighted than Lynceus.

PLUTUS
And how should you be able to do that, you, who are but a mortal?

CHREMYLUS
I have great hope, after the answer Apollo gave me, shaking his sacred laurels the while.

PLUTUS
Is he in the plot then?

CHREMYLUS
Aye, truly.

PLUTUS
Take care what you say.

CHREMYLUS
Never fear, friend; for, be well assured, that if it has to cost me my life, I will carry out what I have in my head.

CARIO
And I will help you, if you permit it.

CHREMYLUS
We shall have many other helpers as well—all the worthy folk who are wanting for bread.

PLUTUS
Ah! ha! they'll prove sorry helpers.

CHREMYLUS
No, not so, once they've grown rich. But you, Cario, run quick ...

CARIO
Where?

CHREMYLUS
... to call my comrades, the other husbandmen, that each of them may come here to take his share of the gifts of Plutus.

CARIO
I'm off. But let someone come from the house to take this morsel of meat. [1]

[1] A part of the victim which Cario was bringing back from the Temple; it was customary to present the remains of a sacrifice to friends and relations.

CHREMYLUS
I'll see to that; you run your hardest. As for you, Plutus, the most excellent of all the gods, come in here with me; this is the house you must fill with riches today, by fair means or foul.

PLUTUS

I don't like at all going into other folks' houses in this manner; I have never got any good from it. If I got inside a miser's house, straightway he would bury me deep underground; if some honest fellow among his friends came to ask him for the smallest coin, he would deny ever having seen me. Then if I went to a fool's house, he would sacrifice me as a prey to gaming and to girls, and very soon I should be completely stripped and pitched out of doors.

CHREMYLUS
That's because you have never met a man who knew how to avoid the two extremes; moderation is the strong point in my character. I love saving as much as anybody, and I know how to spend, when 'tis needed. But let us go in; I want to make you known to my wife and to my only son, whom I love most of all after yourself.

PLUTUS
Aye, after myself, I'm very sure of that.

CHREMYLUS
Why should I hide the truth from you?

CARIO
Come, you active workers, who, like my master, eat nothing but garlic and the poorest food, you who are his friends and his neighbours, hasten your steps, hurry yourselves; there's not a moment to lose; this is the critical hour, when your presence and your support is needed by him.

CHORUS
Why, don't you see we are speeding as fast as men can, who are already enfeebled by age? But do you deem it fitting to make us run like this before ever telling us why your master has called us?

CARIO
I've grown hoarse with the telling, but you won't listen. My master is going to drag you all out of the stupid, sapless life you are leading and ensure you one full of all delights.

CHORUS
And how is he going to manage that?

CARIO
My poor friends, he has brought with him a disgusting old fellow, all bent and wrinkled, with a most pitiful appearance, bald and toothless; upon my word, I even believe he is circumcised like some vile barbarian.

CHORUS
These are news worth their weight in gold! What are you saying? Repeat it to me; no doubt it means he is bringing back a heap of wealth.

CARIO
No, but a heap of all the infirmities attendant on old age.

CHORUS
If you are tricking us, you shall pay us for it. Beware of our sticks!

CARIO
Do you deem me so brazen as all that, and my words mere lies?

CHORUS

What serious airs the rascal puts on! Look! his legs are already shrieking, "oh! oh!" they are asking for the shackles and wedges.

CARIO

'Tis in the tomb that 'tis your lot to judge. Why don't you go there? Charon has given you your ticket.[1]

[1] The citizens appointed to act as dicasts, or jurymen, drew lots each year to decide in which Court they should sit. There were ten Courts, each of which was indicated by one of the first ten letters of the alphabet, and the urn contained as many tickets marked with these letters as there were dicasts. Cario means to say here that the old men of the Chorus should remember that they have soon to die themselves instead of bothering about punishing him.

CHORUS

Plague take you! you cursed rascal, who rail at us and have not even the heart to tell us why your master has made us come. We were pressed for time and tired out, yet we came with all haste, and in our hurry we have passed by lots of wild onions without even gathering them.

CARIO

I will no longer conceal the truth from you. Friends, 'tis Plutus whom my master brings, Plutus, who will give you riches.

CHORUS

What! we shall really all become rich!

CARIO

Aye, certainly; you will then be Midases, provided you grow ass's ears.

CHORUS

What joy, what happiness! If what you tell me is true, I long to dance with delight.

CARIO

And I too, threttanello! I want to imitate Cyclops and lead your troop by stamping like this. Do you, my dear little ones, cry, aye, cry again and bleat forth the plaintive song of the sheep and of the stinking goats; follow me with erected organs like lascivious goats ready for action.

CHORUS

As for us, threttanello! we will seek you, dear Cyclops, bleating, and if we find you with your wallet full of fresh herbs, all disgusting in your filth, sodden with wine and sleeping in the midst of your sheep, we will seize a great flaming stake and burn out your eye.

CARIO

I will copy that Circé of Corinth, whose potent philtres compelled the companions of Philonides to swallow balls of dung, which she herself had kneaded with her hands, as if they were swine; and do you too grunt with joy and follow your mother, my little pigs.

CHORUS

Oh! Circé with the potent philtres, who besmear your companions so filthily, what pleasure I shall have in imitating the son of Laertes! I will hang you up by your testicles, I will rub your nose with dung like a goat, and like Aristyllus you shall say through your half-opened lips, "Follow your mother, my little pigs."

CARIO
Enough of tomfoolery, assume a grave demeanour; unknown to my master I am going to take bread and meat; and when I have fed well, I shall resume my work.

CHREMYLUS
To say, "Hail! my dear neighbours!" is an old form of greeting and well worn with use; so therefore I embrace you, because you have not crept like tortoises, but have come rushing here in all haste. Now help me to watch carefully and closely over the god.

CHORUS
Be at ease. You shall see with what martial zeal I will guard him. What! we jostle each other at the Assembly for three obols, and am I going to let Plutus in person be stolen from me?

CHREMYLUS
But I see Blepsidemus; by his bearing and his haste I can readily see he knows or suspects something.

BLEPSIDEMUS
What has happened then? Whence, how has Chremylus suddenly grown rich? I don't believe a word of it. Nevertheless, nothing but his sudden fortune was being talked about in the barbers' booths. But I am above all surprised that his good fortune has not made him forget his friends; that is not the usual way!

CHREMYLUS
By the gods, Blepsidemus, I will hide nothing from you. To-day things are better than yesterday; let us share, for are you not my friend?

BLEPSIDEMUS
Have you really grown rich as they say?

CHREMYLUS
I shall be soon, if the god agrees to it. But there is still some risk to run.

BLEPSIDEMUS
What risk?

CHREMYLUS
What risk?

BLEPSIDEMUS
What do you mean? Explain.

CHREMYLUS
If we succeed, we are happy for ever, but if we fail, it is all over with us.

BLEPSIDEMUS
'Tis a bad business, and one that doesn't please me! To grow rich all at once and yet to be fearful! ah! I suspect something that's little good.

CHREMYLUS

What do you mean, that's little good?

BLEPSIDEMUS

No doubt you have just stolen some gold and silver from some temple and are repenting.

CHREMYLUS

Nay! heaven preserve me from that!

BLEPSIDEMUS

A truce to idle phrases! the thing is only too apparent, my friend.

CHREMYLUS

Don't suspect such a thing of me.

BLEPSIDEMUS

Alas! then there is no honest man! not one, that can resist the attraction of gold!

CHREMYLUS

By Demeter, you have no common sense.

BLEPSIDEMUS

To have to persist like this in denial one's whole life long!

CHREMYLUS

But, good gods, you are mad, my dear fellow!

BLEPSIDEMUS

His very look is distraught; he has done some crime!

CHREMYLUS

Ah! I know the tune you are playing now; you think I have stolen, and want your share.

BLEPSIDEMUS

My share of what, pray?

CHREMYLUS

You are beside the mark; the thing is quite otherwise.

BLEPSIDEMUS

'Tis perhaps not a theft, but some piece of knavery!

CHREMYLUS

You are insane!

BLEPSIDEMUS

What? You have done no man an injury?

CHREMYLUS

No! assuredly not!

BLEPSIDEMUS

But, great gods, what am I to think? You won't tell me the truth.

CHREMYLUS

You accuse me without really knowing anything.

BLEPSIDEMUS

Listen, friend, no doubt the matter can yet be hushed up, before it gets noised abroad, at trifling expense; I will buy the orators' silence.

CHREMYLUS

Aye, you will lay out three minae and, as my friend, you will reckon twelve against me.

BLEPSIDEMUS

I know someone who will come and seat himself at the foot of the tribunal, holding a supplicant's bough in his hand and surrounded by his wife and children, for all the world like the Heraclidae of Pamphilus.

CHREMYLUS

Not at all, poor fool! But, thanks to me, worthy folk, intelligent and moderate men alone shall be rich henceforth.

BLEPSIDEMUS

What are you saying? Have you then stolen so much as all that?

CHREMYLUS

Oh! your insults will be the death of me.

BLEPSIDEMUS

'Tis rather you yourself who are courting death.

CHREMYLUS

Not so, you wretch, since I have Plutus.

BLEPSIDEMUS

You have Plutus? Which one?

CHREMYLUS

The god himself.

BLEPSIDEMUS

And where is he?

CHREMYLUS

There.

BLEPSIDEMUS

Where?

CHREMYLUS

Indoors.

BLEPSIDEMUS
Indoors?

CHREMYLUS
Aye, certainly.

BLEPSIDEMUS
Get you gone! Plutus in your house?

CHREMYLUS
Yes, by the gods!

BLEPSIDEMUS
Are you telling me the truth?

CHREMYLUS
I am.

BLEPSIDEMUS
Swear it by Hestia.

CHREMYLUS
I swear it by Posidon.

BLEPSIDEMUS
The god of the sea?

CHREMYLUS
Aye, and by all the other Posidons, if such there be.

BLEPSIDEMUS
And you don't send him to us, to your friends?

CHREMYLUS
We've not got to that point yet.

BLEPSIDEMUS
What do you say? Is there no chance of sharing?

CHREMYLUS
Why, no. We must first ...

BLEPSIDEMUS
Do what?

CHREMYLUS
... restore him his sight.

BLEPSIDEMUS
Restore whom his sight? Speak!

CHREMYLUS
PLUTUS
It must be done, no matter how.

BLEPSIDEMUS
Is he then really blind?

CHREMYLUS
Yes, undoubtedly.

BLEPSIDEMUS
I am no longer surprised he never came to me.

CHREMYLUS
And it please the gods, he'll come there now.

BLEPSIDEMUS
Must we not go and seek a physician?

CHREMYLUS
Seek physicians at Athens? Nay! there's no art where there's no fee. [1]

[1] Physicians at Athens were paid very indifferently, and hence the most skilled sought their practice in other cities.

BLEPSIDEMUS
Let's bethink ourselves well.

CHREMYLUS
There is not one.

BLEPSIDEMUS
'Tis a positive fact, I don't know of one.

CHREMYLUS
But I have thought the matter well over, and the best thing is to make Plutus lie in the Temple of Aesculapius.

BLEPSIDEMUS
Aye, unquestionably 'tis the very best thing. Be quick and lead him away to the Temple.

CHREMYLUS
I am going there.

BLEPSIDEMUS
Then hurry yourself.

CHREMYLUS
'Tis just what I am doing.

POVERTY
Unwise, perverse, unholy men! What are you daring to do, you pitiful, wretched mortals? Whither are you flying? Stop! I command it!

BLEPSIDEMUS
Oh! great gods!

POVERTY
My arm shall destroy you, you infamous beings! Such an attempt is not to be borne; neither man nor god has ever dared the like. You shall die!

CHREMYLUS
And who are you? Oh! what a ghastly pallor!

BLEPSIDEMUS
'Tis perchance some Erinnys, some Fury, from the theatre; there's a kind of wild tragedy look in her eyes.

CHREMYLUS
But she has no torch.

BLEPSIDEMUS
Let's knock her down!

POVERTY
Who do you think I am?

CHREMYLUS
Some wine-shop keeper or egg-woman. Otherwise you would not have shrieked so loud at us, who have done nothing to you.

POVERTY
Indeed? And have you not done me the most deadly injury by seeking to banish me from every country?

CHREMYLUS
Why, have you not got the Barathrum [1] left? But who are you? Answer me quickly!

[1] A ravine into which criminals were hurled at Athens.

POVERTY
I am one that will punish you this very day for having wanted to make me disappear from here.

BLEPSIDEMUS
Might it be the tavern-keeper in my neighbourhood, who is always cheating me in measure?

POVERTY
I am Poverty, who have lived with you for so many years.

BLEPSIDEMUS
Oh! great Apollo! oh, ye gods! whither shall I fly?

CHREMYLUS
Now then! what are you doing? You poltroon! Will you kindly stop here?

BLEPSIDEMUS
Not I.

CHREMYLUS
Will you have the goodness to stop. Are two men to fly from a woman?

BLEPSIDEMUS
But, you wretch, 'tis Poverty, the most fearful monster that ever drew breath.

CHREMYLUS
Stay where you are, I beg of you.

BLEPSIDEMUS
No! no! a thousand times, no!

CHREMYLUS
Could we do anything worse than leave the god in the lurch and fly before this woman without so much as ever offering to fight?

BLEPSIDEMUS
But what weapons have we? Are we in a condition to show fight? Where is the breastplate, the buckler, that this wretch has not pledged?

CHREMYLUS
Be at ease. Plutus will readily triumph over her threats unaided.

POVERTY
Dare you reply, you scoundrels, you who are caught red-handed at the most horrible crime?

CHREMYLUS
As for you, you cursed jade, you pursue me with your abuse, though I have never done you the slightest harm.

POVERTY
Do you think it is doing me no harm to restore Plutus to the use of his eyes?

CHREMYLUS
Is this doing you harm, that we shower blessings on all men?

POVERTY
And what do you think will ensure their happiness?

CHREMYLUS
Ah! first of all we shall drive you out of Greece.

POVERTY
Drive me out? Could you do mankind a greater harm?

CHREMYLUS
Yes—if I gave up my intention to deliver them from you.

POVERTY
Well, let us discuss this point first. I propose to show that I am the sole cause of all your blessings, and that your safety depends on me alone. If I don't succeed, then do what you like to me.

CHREMYLUS
How dare you talk like this, you impudent hussy?

POVERTY
Agree to hear me and I think it will be very easy for me to prove that you are entirely on the wrong road, when you want to make the just men wealthy.

BLEPSIDEMUS
Oh! cudgel and rope's end, come to my help!

POVERTY
Why such wrath and these shouts, before you hear my arguments?

BLEPSIDEMUS
But who could listen to such words without exclaiming?

POVERTY
Any man of sense.

CHREMYLUS
But if you lose your case, what punishment will you submit to?

POVERTY
Choose what you will.

CHREMYLUS
That's all right.

POVERTY
You shall suffer the same if you are beaten!

CHREMYLUS
Do you think twenty deaths a sufficiently large stake?

BLEPSIDEMUS
Good enough for her, but for us two would suffice.

POVERTY
You won't escape, for is there indeed a single valid argument to oppose me with?

CHORUS
To beat her in this debate, you must call upon all your wits. Make no allowances and show no weakness!

CHREMYLUS

It is right that the good should be happy, that the wicked and the impious, on the other hand, should be miserable; that is a truth, I believe, which no one will gainsay. To realize this condition of things is as great a proposal as it is noble and useful in every respect, and we have found a means of attaining the object of our wishes. If Plutus recovers his sight and ceases from wandering about unseeing and at random, he will go to seek the just men and never leave them again; he will shun the perverse and ungodly; so, thanks to him, all men will become honest, rich and pious. Can anything better be conceived for the public weal?

BLEPSIDEMUS

Of a certainty, no! I bear witness to that. It is not even necessary she should reply.

CHREMYLUS

Does it not seem that everything is extravagance in the world, or rather madness, when you watch the way things go? A crowd of rogues enjoy blessings they have won by sheer injustice, while more honest folks are miserable, die of hunger, and spend their whole lives with you.

CHORUS

Yes, if Plutus became clear-sighted again and drove out Poverty, 'twould be the greatest blessing possible for the human race.

POVERTY

Here are two old men, whose brains are easy to confuse, who assist each other to talk rubbish and drivel to their hearts' content. But if your wishes were realized, your profit would be great! Let Plutus recover his sight and divide his favours out equally to all, and none will ply either trade or art any longer; all toil would be done away with. Who would wish to hammer iron, build ships, sew, turn, cut up leather, bake bricks, bleach linen, tan hides, or break up the soil of the earth with the plough and garner the gifts of Demeter, if he could live in idleness and free from all this work?

CHREMYLUS

What nonsense all this is! All these trades which you just mention will be plied by our slaves.

POVERTY

Your slaves! And by what means will these slaves be got?

CHREMYLUS

We will buy them.

POVERTY

But first say, who will sell them, if everyone is rich?

CHREMYLUS

Some greedy dealer from Thessaly—the land which supplies so many.

POVERTY

But if your system is applied, there won't be a single slave-dealer left. What rich man would risk his life to devote himself to this traffic? You will have to toil, to dig and submit yourself to all kinds of hard labour; so that your life would be more wretched even than it is now.

CHREMYLUS

May this prediction fall upon yourself!

POVERTY
You will not be able to sleep in a bed, for no more will ever be manufactured; nor on carpets, for who would weave them if he had gold? When you bring a young bride to your dwelling, you will have no essences wherewith to perfume her, nor rich embroidered cloaks dyed with dazzling colours in which to clothe her. And yet what is the use of being rich, if you are to be deprived of all these enjoyments? On the other hand, you have all that you need in abundance, thanks to me; to the artisan I am like a severe mistress, who forces him by need and poverty to seek the means of earning his livelihood.

CHREMYLUS
And what good thing can you give us, unless it be burns in the bath, and swarms of brats and old women who cry with hunger, and clouds uncountable of lice, gnats and flies, which hover about the wretch's head, trouble him, awake him and say, "You will be hungry, but get up!" Besides, to possess a rag in place of a mantle, a pallet of rushes swarming with bugs, that do not let you close your eyes for a bed; a rotten piece of matting for a coverlet; a big stone for a pillow, on which to lay your head; to eat mallow roots instead of bread, and leaves of withered radish instead of cake; to have nothing but the cover of a broken jug for a stool, the stave of a cask, and broken at that, for a kneading-trough, that is the life you make for us! Are these the mighty benefits with which you pretend to load mankind?

POVERTY
'Tis not my life that you describe; you are attacking the existence beggars lead.

CHREMYLUS
Is beggary not Poverty's sister?

POVERTY
Thrasybulus and Dionysius are one and the same according to you. No, my life is not like that and never will be. The beggar, whom you have depicted to us, never possesses anything. The poor man lives thriftily and attentive to his work; he has not got too much, but he does not lack what he really needs.

CHREMYLUS
Oh! what a happy life, by Demeter! to live sparingly, to toil incessantly and not to leave enough to pay for a tomb!

POVERTY
That's it! Jest, jeer, and never talk seriously! But what you don't know is this, that men with me are worth more, both in mind and body, than with Plutus. With him they are gouty, big-bellied, heavy of limb and scandalously stout; with me they are thin, wasp-waisted, and terrible to the foe.

CHREMYLUS
'Tis no doubt by starving them that you give them that waspish waist.

POVERTY
As for behaviour, I will prove to you that modesty dwells with me and insolence with Plutus.

CHREMYLUS
Oh! the sweet modesty of stealing and breaking through walls.

BLEPSIDEMUS

Aye, the thief is truly modest, for he hides himself.

POVERTY

Look at the orators in our republics; as long as they are poor, both State and people can only praise their uprightness; but once they are fattened on the public funds, they conceive a hatred for justice, plan intrigues against the people and attack the democracy.

CHREMYLUS

That is absolutely true, although your tongue is very vile. But it matters not, so don't put on those triumphant airs; you shall not be punished any the less for having tried to persuade me that poverty is worth more than wealth.

POVERTY

Not being able to refute my arguments, you chatter at random and exert yourself to no purpose.

CHREMYLUS

Then tell me this, why does all mankind flee from you?

POVERTY

Because I make them better. Children do the very same; they flee from the wise counsels of their fathers. So difficult is it to see one's true interest.

CHREMYLUS

Will you say that Zeus cannot discern what is best? Well, he takes Plutus to himself ...

BLEPSIDEMUS

... and banishes Poverty to earth.

POVERTY

Ah me! how purblind you are, you old fellows of the days of Saturn! Why, Zeus is poor, and I will clearly prove it to you. In the Olympic games, which he founded, and to which he convokes the whole of Greece every four years, why does he only crown the victorious athletes with wild olive? If he were rich he would give them gold.

CHREMYLUS

'Tis in that way he shows that he clings to his wealth; he is sparing with it, won't part with any portion of it, only bestows baubles on the victors and keeps his money for himself.

POVERTY

But wealth coupled to such sordid greed is yet more shameful than poverty.

CHREMYLUS

May Zeus destroy you, both you and your chaplet of wild olive!

POVERTY

Thus you dare to maintain that poverty is not the fount of all blessings!

CHREMYLUS

Ask Hecaté [1] whether it is better to be rich or starving; she will tell you that the rich send her a meal every month and that the poor make it disappear before it is even served. But go and hang yourself and don't breathe another syllable. I will not be convinced against my will.

[1] The ancients placed statues of Hecaté at the cross-roads ([Greek: triodoi], places where three roads meet), because of the three names, Artemis, Phoebé and Hecaté, under which the same goddess was worshipped. On the first day of the month the rich had meals served before these statues and invited the poor to them.

POVERTY
"Oh! citizens of Argos! do you hear what he says?"

CHREMYLUS
Invoke Pauson, your boon companion, rather.

POVERTY
Alas! what is to become of me?

CHREMYLUS
Get you gone, be off quick and a pleasant journey to you.

POVERTY
But where shall I go?

CHREMYLUS
To gaol; but hurry up, let us put an end to this.

POVERTY
One day you will recall me.

CHREMYLUS
Then you can return; but disappear for the present. I prefer to be rich; you are free to knock your head against the walls in your rage.

BLEPSIDEMUS
And I too welcome wealth. I want, when I leave the bath all perfumed with essences, to feast bravely with my wife and children and to break wind in the faces of toilers and Poverty.

CHREMYLUS
So that hussy has gone at last! But let us make haste to put Plutus to bed in the Temple of Aesculapius.

BLEPSIDEMUS
Let us make haste; else some bothering fellow may again come to interrupt us.

CHREMYLUS
Cario, bring the coverlets and all that I have got ready from the house; let us conduct the god to the Temple, taking care to observe all the proper rites.

CHORUS
[Text Missing.] [1]

[1] *There is here a long interval of time, during which Plutus is taken to the Temple of Aesculapius and cured of his blindness. In the first edition probably the Parabasis came in here; at all events a long choral ode must have intervened.*

CARIO

Oh! you old fellows, who used to dip out the broth served to the poor at the festival of Theseus with little pieces of bread hollowed like a spoon, how worthy of envy is your fate! How happy you are, both you and all just men!

CHORUS

My good fellow, what has happened to your friends? You seem the bearer of good tidings.

CARIO

What joy for my master and even more for Plutus! The god has regained his sight; his eyes sparkle with the greatest brilliancy, thanks to the benevolent care of Aesculapius.

CHORUS

Oh! what transports of joy! oh! What shouts of gladness!

CARIO

Aye! one is compelled to rejoice, whether one will or not.

CHORUS

I will sing to the honour of Aesculapius, the son of illustrious Zeus, with a resounding voice; he is the beneficent star which men adore.

CHREMYLUS' WIFE

What mean these shouts? Is there good news. With what impatience have I been waiting in the house, and for so long too!

CARIO

Quick! quick! some wine, mistress. And drink yourself, for 'tis much to your taste; I bring you all blessings in a lump.

WIFE

Where are they?

CARIO

In my words, as you are going to see.

WIFE

Have done with trifling! come, speak.

CARIO

Listen, I am going to tell you everything from the feet to the head.

WIFE

Ah! don't throw anything at my head.

CARIO

Not even the happiness that has come to you?

WIFE
No, no, nothing ... to annoy me.

CARIO
Having arrived near to the Temple with our patient, then so unfortunate, but now at the apex of happiness, of blessedness, we first led him down to the sea to purify him.

WIFE
Ah! what a singular pleasure for an old man to bathe in the cold sea-water!

CARIO
Then we repaired to the Temple of the god. Once the wafers and the various offerings had been consecrated upon the altar, and the cake of wheaten-meal had been handed over to the devouring Hephaestus, we made Plutus lie on a couch according to the rite, and each of us prepared himself a bed of leaves.

WIFE
Had any other folk come to beseech the deity?

CARIO
Yes. Firstly, Neoclides, who is blind, but steals much better than those who see clearly; then many others attacked by complaints of all kinds. The lights were put out and the priest enjoined us to sleep, especially recommending us to keep silent should we hear any noise. There we were all lying down quite quietly. I could not sleep; I was thinking of a certain stew-pan full of pap placed close to an old woman and just behind her head. I had a furious longing to slip towards that side. But just as I was lifting my head, I noticed the priest, who was sweeping off both the cakes and the figs on the sacred table; then he made the round of the altars and sanctified the cakes that remained, by stowing them away in a bag. I therefore resolved to follow such a pious example and made straight for the pap.

WIFE
You wretch! and had you no fear of the god?

CARIO
Aye, indeed! I feared that the god with his crown on his head might have been near the stew-pan before me. I said to myself, "Like priest, like god." On hearing the noise I made, the old woman put out her hand, but I hissed and bit it, just as a sacred serpent might have done. Quick she drew back her hand, slipped down into the bed with her head beneath the coverlets and never moved again; only she let go some wind in her fear which stunk worse than a weasel. As for myself, I swallowed a goodly portion of the pap and, having made a good feed, went back to bed.

WIFE
And did not the god come?

CAIRO
He did not tarry; and when he was near us, oh! dear! such a good joke happened. My belly was quite blown out, and I let wind with the loudest of noises.

WIFE

Doubtless the god pulled a wry face?

CARIO
No, but Iaso blushed a little and Panacea turned her head away, holding her nose; for my perfume is not that of roses.

WIFE
And what did the god do?

CARIO
He paid not the slightest heed.

WIFE
He must then be a pretty coarse kind of god?

CARIO
I don't say that, but he's used to tasting shit.

WIFE
Impudent knave, go on with you!

CARIO
Then I hid myself in my bed all a-tremble. Aesculapius did the round of the patients and examined them all with great attention; then a slave placed beside him a stone mortar, a pestle and a little box.

WIFE
Of stone?

CARIO
No, not of stone.

WIFE
But how could you see all this, you arch-rascal, when you say you were hiding all the time?

CARIO
Why, great gods, through my cloak, for 'tis not without holes! He first prepared an ointment for Neoclides; he threw three heads of Tenian garlic into the mortar, pounded them with an admixture of fig-tree sap and lentisk, moistened the whole with Sphettian vinegar, and, turning back the patient's eyelids, applied his salve to the interior of the eyes, so that the pain might be more excruciating. Neoclides shrieked, howled, sprang towards the foot of his bed and wanted to bolt, but the god laughed and said to him, "Keep where you are with your salve; by doing this you will not go and perjure yourself before the Assembly."

WIFE
What a wise god and what a friend to our city!

CARIO
Thereupon he came and seated himself at the head of Plutus' bed, took a perfectly clean rag and wiped his eye-lids; Panacea covered his head and face with a purple cloth, while the god whistled, and two enormous snakes came rushing from the sanctuary.

WIFE
Great gods!

CARIO
They slipped gently beneath the purple cloth and, as far as I could judge, licked the patient's eyelids; for, in less time than even you need, mistress, to drain down ten beakers of wine, Plutus rose up; he could see. I clapped my hands with joy and awoke my master, and the god immediately disappeared with the serpents into the sanctuary. As for those who were lying near Plutus, you can imagine that they embraced him tenderly. Dawn broke and not one of them had closed an eye. As for myself, I did not cease thanking the god who had so quickly restored to Plutus his sight and had made Neoclides blinder than ever.

WIFE
Oh! thou great Aesculapius! How mighty is thy power! [To **CARIO**] But tell me, where is Plutus now?

CARIO
He is approaching, escorted by an immense crowd. The rich, whose wealth is ill-gotten, are knitting their brows and shooting at him looks of fierce hate, while the just folk, who led a wretched existence, embrace him and grasp his hand in the transport of their joy; they follow in his wake, their heads wreathed with garlands, laughing and blessing their deliverer; the old men make the earth resound as they walk together keeping time. Come, all of you, all, down to the very least, dance, leap and form yourselves into a chorus; no longer do you risk being told, when you go home, "There is no meal in the bag."

WIFE
And I, by Hecate! I will string you a garland of cakes for the good tidings you have brought me.

CARIO
Hurry, make haste then; our friends are close at hand.

WIFE
I will go indoors to fetch some gifts of welcome, to celebrate these eyes that have just been opened.

CARIO
Meantime I am going forth to meet them.

CHORUS
[Text Missing.]

PLUTUS
I adore thee, oh! thou divine sun, and thee I greet thou city, the beloved of Pallas; be welcome, thou land of Cecrops, which hast received me. Alas! what manner of men I associated with! I blush to think of it. While, on the other hand, I shunned those who deserved my friendship; I knew neither the vices of the ones nor the virtues of the others. A twofold mistake, and in both cases equally fatal! Ah! what a misfortune was mine! But I want to change everything; and in future I mean to prove to mankind that, if I gave to the wicked, 'twas against my will.

CHREMYLUS [To the **CROWD** who impede him]

Get you gone! Oh! what a lot of friends spring into being when you are fortunate! They dig me with their elbows and bruise my shins to prove their affection. Each one wants to greet me. What a crowd of old fellows thronged round me on the market-place!

WIFE
Oh! thou, who art dearest of all to me, and thou too, be welcome! Allow me, Plutus, to shower these gifts of welcome over you in due accord with custom.

PLUTUS
No. This is the first house I enter after having regained my sight; I shall take nothing from it, for 'tis my place rather to give.

WIFE
Do you refuse these gifts?

PLUTUS
I will accept them at your fireside, as custom requires. Besides, we shall thus avoid a ridiculous scene; it is not meet that the poet should throw dried figs and dainties to the spectators; 'tis a vulgar trick to make 'em laugh.

WIFE
You are right. Look! yonder's Dexinicus, who was already getting to his feet to catch the figs as they flew past him.

CHORUS
[Text Missing.]

CARIO
How pleasant it is, friends, to live well, especially when it costs nothing! What a deluge of blessings flood our household, and that too without our having wronged ever a soul! Ah! what a delightful thing is wealth! The bin is full of white flour and the wine-jars run over with fragrant liquor; all the chests are crammed with gold and silver, 'tis a sight to see; the tank is full of oil, the phials with perfumes, and the garret with dried figs. Vinegar flasks, plates, stew-pots and all the platters are of brass; our rotten old wooden trenchers for the fish have to-day become dishes of silver; the very night-commode is of ivory. We others, the slaves, we play at odd and even with gold pieces, and carry luxury so far that we no longer wipe ourselves with stones, but use garlic stalks instead. My master, at this moment, is crowned with flowers and sacrificing a pig, a goat and a ram; 'tis the smoke that has driven me out, for I could no longer endure it, it hurt my eyes so.

A JUST MAN
Come, my child, come with me. Let us go and find the god.

CHREMYLUS
Who comes here?

JUST MAN
A man who was once wretched, but now is happy.

CHREMYLUS
A just man then?

JUST MAN

You have it.

CHREMYLUS

Well! what do you want?

JUST MAN

I come to thank the god for all the blessings he has showered on me. My father had left me a fairly decent fortune, and I helped those of my friends who were in want; 'twas, to my thinking, the most useful thing I could do with my fortune.

CHREMYLUS

And you were quickly ruined?

JUST MAN

Entirely.

CHREMYLUS

Since then you have been living in misery?

JUST MAN

In truth I have; I thought I could count, in case of need, upon the friends whose property I had helped, but they turned their backs upon me and pretended not to see me.

CHREMYLUS

They laughed at you, 'tis evident.

JUST MAN

Just so. With my empty coffers, I had no more friends.

CHREMYLUS

But your lot has changed.

JUST MAN

Yes, and so I come to the god to make him the acts of gratitude that are his due.

CHREMYLUS

But with what object now do you bring this old cloak, which your slave is carrying? Tell me.

JUST MAN

I wish to dedicate it to the god.

CHREMYLUS

Were you initiated into the Great Mysteries in that cloak?

JUST MAN

No, but I shivered in it for thirteen years.

CHREMYLUS

And this footwear?

JUST MAN
These also are my winter companions.

CHREMYLUS
And you wish to dedicate them too?

JUST MAN
Unquestionably.

CHREMYLUS
Fine presents to offer to the god!

AN INFORMER
Alas! alas! I am a lost man. Ah! thrice, four, five, twelve times, or rather ten thousand times unhappy fate! Why, why must fortune deal me such rough blows?

CHREMYLUS
Oh, Apollo, my tutelary! oh! ye favourable gods! what has overtaken this man?

INFORMER
Ah! am I not deserving of pity? I have lost everything; this cursed god has stripped me bare. Ah! if there be justice in heaven, he shall be struck blind again.

JUST MAN
Methinks I know what's the matter. If this man is unfortunate, 'tis because he's of little account and small honesty; and i' faith he looks it too.

CHREMYLUS
Then, by Zeus! his plight is but just.

INFORMER
He promised that if he recovered his sight, he would enrich us all unaided; whereas he has ruined more than one.

CHREMYLUS
But whom has he thus ill-used?

INFORMER
Me.

CHREMYLUS
You were doubtless a villainous thief then.

INFORMER [To **CHREMYLUS** and **CARIO**]
'Tis rather you yourselves who were such wretches; I am certain you have got my money.

CHREMYLUS
Ha! by Demeter! 'tis an informer. What impudence!

CARIO
He's ravenously hungry, that's certain.

INFORMER
You shall follow me this very instant to the marketplace, where the torture of the wheel shall force the confession of your misdeeds from you.

CARIO
Ha! look out for yourself!

JUST MAN
By Zeus the Deliverer, what gratitude all Greeks owe to Plutus, if he destroys these vile informers!

INFORMER
You are laughing at me. Ho! ho! I denounce you as their accomplice. Where did you steal that new cloak from? Yesterday I saw you with one utterly worn out.

JUST MAN
I fear you not, thanks to this ring, for which I paid Eudemus a drachma.

CHREMYLUS
Ah! there's no ring to preserve you from the informer's bite.

INFORMER
The insolent wretches! But, my fine jokers, you have not told me what you are up to here. Nothing good, I'll be bound.

CHREMYLUS
Nothing of any good for you, be sure of that.

INFORMER
By Zeus! you're going to dine at my expense!

CHREMYLUS
You vile impostor, may you burst with an empty belly, both you and your witness.

INFORMER
You deny it? I reckon, you villians, that there is much salt fish and roast meat in this house. Hu! hu! hu! hu! hu! hu!

[He sniffs.]

CHREMYLUS
Can you smell anything, rascal?

INFORMER
Can such outrages be borne, oh, Zeus! Ye gods! how cruel it is to see me treated thus, when I am such an honest fellow and such a good citizen!

CHREMYLUS
You an honest man! you a good citizen!

INFORMER

A better one than any.

CHREMYLUS
Ah! well then, answer my questions.

INFORMER
Concerning what?

CHREMYLUS
Are you a husbandman?

INFORMER
D'ye take me for a fool?

CHREMYLUS
A merchant?

INFORMER
I assume the title, when it serves me.[1]

[1] The merchants engaged in maritime commerce were absolved from military service.

CHREMYLUS
Do you ply any trade?

INFORMER
No, most assuredly not!

CHREMYLUS
Then how do you live, if you do nothing?

INFORMER
I superintend public and private business.

CHREMYLUS
You! And by what right, pray?

INFORMER
Because it pleases me to do so.

CHREMYLUS
Like a thief you sneak yourself in where you have no business. You are hated by all and you claim to be an honest man?

INFORMER
What, you fool? I have not the right to dedicate myself entirely to my country's service?

CHREMYLUS
Is the country served by vile intrigue?

INFORMER

It is served by watching that the established law is observed—by allowing no one to violate it.

CHREMYLUS
That's the duty of the tribunals; they are established to that end.

INFORMER
And who is the prosecutor before the dicasts?

CHREMYLUS
Whoever wishes to be.

INFORMER
Well then, 'tis I who choose to be prosecutor; and thus all public affairs fall within my province.

CHREMYLUS
I pity Athens for being in such vile clutches. But would you not prefer to live quietly and free from all care and anxiety?

INFORMER
To do nothing is to live an animal's life.

CHREMYLUS
Thus you will not change your mode of life?

INFORMER
No, though they gave me Plutus himself and the silphium of Battus.

CHREMYLUS [To the **INFORMER**]
Come, quick, off with your cloak.

CARIO
Hi! friend! 'tis you they are speaking to.

CHREMYLUS
Off with your shoes.

CARIO
All this is addressed to you.

INFORMER
Very well! let one of you come near me, if he dares.

CARIO
I dare.

INFORMER
Alas! I am robbed of my clothes in full daylight.

CARIO
That's what comes of meddling with other folk's business and living at their expense.

INFORMER [To his **WITNESS**]
You see what is happening; I call you to witness.

CHREMYLUS
Look how the witness whom you brought is taking to his heels.

INFORMER
Great gods! I am all alone and they assault me.

CARIO
Shout away!

INFORMER
Oh! woe, woe is me!

CARIO
Give me that old ragged cloak, that I may dress out the informer

JUST MAN
No, no; I have dedicated it to Plutus.

CARIO
And where would your offering be better bestowed than on the shoulders of a rascal and a thief? To Plutus fine, rich cloaks should be given.

JUST MAN
And what then shall be done with these shoes? Tell me.

CARIO
I will nail them to his brow as gifts are nailed to the trunks of the wild olive.

INFORMER
I'm off, for you are the strongest, I own. But if I find someone to join me, let him be as weak as he will, I will summon this god, who thinks himself so strong, before the Court this very day, and denounce him as manifestly guilty of overturning the democracy by his will alone and without the consent of the Senate or the popular Assembly.

JUST MAN
Now that you are rigged out from head to foot with my old clothes, hasten to the bath and stand there in the front row to warm yourself better; 'tis the place I formerly had.

CHREMYLUS
Ah! the bath-man would grip you by the testicles and fling you through the door; he would only need to see you to appraise you at your true value.... But let us go in, friend, that you may address your thanksgivings to the god.

CHORUS
[Text Missing.]

AN OLD WOMAN
Dear old men, am I near the house where the new god lives, or have I missed the road?

CHORUS
You are at his door, my pretty little maid, who question us so sweetly.

OLD WOMAN
Then I will summon someone in the house.

CHREMYLUS
'Tis needless! I am here myself. But what matter brings you here?

OLD WOMAN
Ah! a cruel, unjust fate! My dear friend, this god has made life unbearable to me through ceasing to be blind.

CHREMYLUS
What does this mean? Can you be a female informer?

OLD WOMAN
Most certainly not.

CHREMYLUS
Have you not drunk up your money then?

OLD WOMAN
You are mocking me! Nay! I am being devoured with a consuming fire.

CHREMYLUS
Then tell me what is consuming you so fiercely.

OLD WOMAN
Listen! I loved a young man, who was poor, but so handsome, so well-built, so honest! He readily gave way to all I desired and acquitted himself so well! I, for my part, refused him nothing.

CHREMYLUS
And what did he generally ask of you.

OLD WOMAN
Very little; he bore himself towards me with astonishing discretion! perchance twenty drachmae for a cloak or eight for footwear; sometimes he begged me to buy tunics for his sisters or a little mantle for his mother; at times he needed four bushels of corn.

CHREMYLUS
'Twas very little, in truth; I admire his modesty.

OLD WOMAN
And 'twas not as a reward for his complacency that he ever asked me for anything, but as a matter of pure friendship; a cloak I had given would remind him from whom he had got it.

CHREMYLUS
'Twas a fellow who loved you madly.

OLD WOMAN
But 'tis no longer so, for the faithless wretch has sadly altered! I had sent him this cake with the sweetmeats you see here on this dish and let him know that I would visit him in the evening....

CHREMYLUS
Well?

OLD WOMAN
He sent me back my presents and added this tart to them, on condition that I never set foot in his house again. Besides, he sent me this message, "Once upon a time the Milesians were brave."[1]

[1] A proverb, meaning, "All things change with time."

CHREMYLUS
An honest lad, indeed! But what would you? When poor, he would devour anything; now he is rich, he no longer cares for lentils.

OLD WOMAN
Formerly he came to me every day.

CHREMYLUS
To see if you were being buried?

OLD WOMAN
No! he longed to hear the sound of my voice.

CHREMYLUS
And to carry off some present.

OLD WOMAN
If I was downcast, he would call me his little duck or his little dove in a most tender manner....

CHREMYLUS
And then would ask for the wherewithal to buy a pair of shoes.

OLD WOMAN
When I was at the Mysteries of Eleusis in a carriage, someone looked at me; he was so jealous that he beat me the whole of that day.

CHREMYLUS
'Twas because he liked to feed alone.

OLD WOMAN
He told me I had very beautiful hands.

CHREMYLUS
Aye, no doubt, when they handed him twenty drachmae.

OLD WOMAN
That my whole body breathed a sweet perfume.

CHREMYLUS
Yes, like enough, if you poured him out Thasian wine.

OLD WOMAN
That my glance was gentle and charming.

CHREMYLUS
'Twas no fool. He knew how to drag drachmae from a hot-blooded old woman.

OLD WOMAN
Ah! the god has done very, very wrong, saying he would support the victims of injustice.

CHREMYLUS
Well, what must he do? Speak, and it shall be done.

OLD WOMAN
'Tis right to compel him, whom I have loaded with benefits, to repay them in his turn; if not, he does not merit the least of the god's favours.

CHREMYLUS
And did he not do this every night?

OLD WOMAN
He swore he would never leave me, as long as I lived.

CHREMYLUS
Aye, rightly; but he thinks you are no longer alive.

OLD WOMAN
Ah! friend, I am pining away with grief.

CHREMYLUS
You are rotting away, it seems to me.

OLD WOMAN
I have grown so thin, I could slip through a ring.

CHREMYLUS
Yes, if 'twere as large as the hoop of a sieve.

OLD WOMAN
But here is the youth, the cause of my complaint; he looks as though he were going to a festival.

CHREMYLUS
Yes, if his chaplet and his torch are any guides.

YOUTH
Greeting to you.

OLD WOMAN
What does he say?

YOUTH
My ancient old dear, you have grown white very quickly, by heaven!

OLD WOMAN
Oh! what an insult!

CHREMYLUS
It is a long time, then, since he saw you?

OLD WOMAN
A long time? My god! he was with me yesterday.

CHREMYLUS
It must be, then, that, unlike other people, he sees more clearly when he's drunk.

OLD WOMAN
No, but I have always known him for an insolent fellow.

YOUTH
Oh! divine Posidon! Oh, ye gods of old age! what wrinkles she has on her face!

OLD WOMAN
Oh! oh! keep your distance with that torch.

CHREMYLUS
Yes, 'twould be as well; if a single spark were to reach her, she would catch alight like an old olive branch.

YOUTH
I propose to have a game with you.

OLD WOMAN
Where, naughty boy?

YOUTH
Here. Take some nuts in your hand.

OLD WOMAN
What game is this?

YOUTH
Let's play at guessing how many teeth you have.

CHREMYLUS
Ah! I'll tell you; she's got three, or perhaps four.

YOUTH
Pay up; you've lost! she has only one single grinder.

OLD WOMAN

You wretch! you're not in your right senses. Do you insult me thus before this crowd?

YOUTH
I am washing you thoroughly; 'tis doing you a service.

CHREMYLUS
No, no! as she is there, she can still deceive; but if this white-lead is washed off, her wrinkles would come out plainly.

OLD WOMAN
You are only an old fool!

YOUTH
Ah! he is playing the gallant, he is fondling your breasts, and thinks I do not see it.

OLD WOMAN
Oh! no, by Aphrodité, no, you naughty jealous fellow.

CHREMYLUS
Oh! most certainly not, by Hecaté! Verily and indeed I would need to be mad! But, young man, I cannot forgive you, if you cast off this beautiful child.

YOUTH
Why, I adore her.

CHREMYLUS
But nevertheless she accuses you ...

YOUTH
Accuses me of what?

CHREMYLUS
... of having told her insolently, "Once upon a time the Milesians were brave."

YOUTH
Oh! I shall not dispute with you about her.

CHREMYLUS
Why not?

YOUTH
Out of respect for your age; with anyone but you, I should not be so easy; come, take the girl and be happy.

CHREMYLUS
I see, I see; you don't want her any more.

OLD WOMAN
Nay! this is a thing that cannot be allowed.

YOUTH

I cannot argue with a woman, who has been making love these thirteen thousand years.

CHREMYLUS
Yet, since you liked the wine, you should now consume the lees.

YOUTH
But these lees are quite rancid and fusty.

CHREMYLUS
Pass them through a straining-cloth; they'll clarify.

YOUTH
But I want to go in with you to offer these chaplets to the god.

OLD WOMAN
And I too have something to tell him.

YOUTH
Then I don't enter.

CHREMYLUS
Come, have no fear; she won't harm you.

YOUTH
'Tis true; I've been managing the old bark long enough.

OLD WOMAN
Go in; I'll follow after you.

CHREMYLUS
Good gods! that old hag has fastened herself to her youth like a limpet to its rock.

CARIO [Opening the door]
Who knocks at the door? Halloa! I see no one; 'twas then by chance it gave forth that plaintive tone.

HERMES [To **CARIO**, who is about to close the door]
Cario! stop!

CARIO
Eh! friend, was it you who knocked so loudly? Tell me.

HERMES
No, I was going to knock and you forestalled me by opening. Come, call your master quick, then his wife and his children, then his slave and his dog, then thyself and his pig.

CARIO
And what's it all about?

HERMES
It's about this, rascal! Zeus wants to serve you all with the same sauce and hurl the lot of you into the Barathrum.

CARIO

Have a care for your tongue, you bearer of ill tidings! But why does he want to treat us in that scurvy fashion?

HERMES

Because you have committed the most dreadful crime. Since Plutus has recovered his sight, there is nothing for us other gods, neither incense, nor laurels, nor cakes, nor victims, nor anything in the world.

CARIO

And you will never be offered anything more; you governed us too ill.

HERMES

I care nothing at all about the other gods, but 'tis myself. I tell you I am dying of hunger.

CARIO

That's reasoning like a wise fellow.

HERMES

Formerly, from earliest dawn, I was offered all sorts of good things in the wine-shops,—wine-cakes, honey, dried figs, in short, dishes worthy of hermes. Now, I lie the livelong day on my back, with my legs in the air, famishing.

CARIO

And quite right too, for you often had them punished who treated you so well.

HERMES

Ah! the lovely cake they used to knead for me on the fourth of the month!

CARIO

You recall it vainly; your regrets are useless! there'll be no more cake.

HERMES

Ah! the ham I was wont to devour!

CARIO

Well then! make use of your legs and hop on one leg upon the wine-skin,[1] to while away the time.

[1] This game, which was customary during the feasts of Bacchus' consisted in hopping on one leg upon a wine-skin that was blown out and well greased with oil; the competitor who kept his footing longest on one leg, gained the prize.

HERMES

Oh! the grilled entrails I used to swallow down!

CARIO

Your own have got the colic, methinks.

HERMES

Oh! the delicious tipple, half wine, half water!

CARIO

Here, swallow that and be off.

[He discharges a fart.]

HERMES

Would you do a friend a service?

CARIO

Willingly, if I can.

HERMES

Give me some well-baked bread and a big hunk of the victims they are sacrificing in your house.

CARIO

That would be stealing.

HERMES

Do you forget, then, how I used to take care he knew nothing about it when you were stealing something from your master?

CARIO

Because I used to share it with you, you rogue; some cake or other always came your way.

HERMES

Which afterwards you ate up all by yourself.

CARIO

But then you did not share the blows when I was caught.

HERMES

Forget past injuries, now you have taken Phylé. Ah! how I should like to live with you! Take pity and receive me.

CARIO

You would leave the gods to stop here?

HERMES

One is much better off among you.

CARIO

What! you would desert! Do you think that is honest?

HERMES

"Where I live well, there is my country."

CARIO

But how could we employ you here?

HERMES

Place me near the door; I am the watchman god and would shift off the robbers.

CARIO
Shift off! Ah! but we have no love for shifts.

HERMES
Entrust me with business dealings.

CARIO
But we are rich; why should we keep a haggling Hermes?

HERMES
Let me intrigue for you.

CARIO
No, no, intrigues are forbidden; we believe in good faith.

HERMES
I will work for you as a guide.

CARIO
But the god sees clearly now, so we no longer want a guide.

HERMES
Well then, I will preside over the games. Ah! what can you object to in that? Nothing is fitter for Plutus than to give scenic and gymnastic games.

CARIO
How useful 'tis to have so many names! Here you have found the means of earning your bread. I don't wonder the jurymen so eagerly try to get entered for many tribunals.

HERMES
So then, you admit me on these terms.

CARIO
Go and wash the entrails of the victims at the well, so that you may show yourself serviceable at once.

A PRIEST OF ZEUS
Can anyone direct me where Chremylus is?

CHREMYLUS
What would you with him, friend?

PRIEST
Much ill. Since Plutus has recovered his sight, I am perishing of starvation; I, the priest of Zeus the Deliverer, have nothing to eat!

CHREMYLUS
And what is the cause of that, pray?

PRIEST
No one dreams of offering sacrifices.

CHREMYLUS
Why not?

PRIEST
Because all men are rich. Ah! when they had nothing, the merchant who escaped from shipwreck, the accused who was acquitted, all immolated victims; another would sacrifice for the success of some wish and the priest joined in at the feast; but now there is not the smallest victim, not one of the faithful in the temple, but thousands who come there to ease themselves.

CHREMYLUS
Don't you take your share of those offerings?

PRIEST
Hence I think I too am going to say good-bye to Zeus the Deliverer, and stop here myself.

CHREMYLUS
Be at ease, all will go well, if it so please the god. Zeus the Deliverer is here; he came of his own accord.

PRIEST
Ha! that's good news.

CHREMYLUS
Wait a little; we are going to install Plutus presently in the place he formerly occupied behind the Temple of Athené; there he will watch over our treasures for ever. But let lighted torches be brought; take these and walk in solemn procession in front of the god.

PRIEST
That's magnificent!

CHREMYLUS
Let Plutus be summoned.

OLD WOMAN
And I, what am I to do?

CHREMYLUS
Take the pots of vegetables which we are going to offer to the god in honour of his installation and carry them on your head; you just happen luckily to be wearing a beautiful embroidered robe.

OLD WOMAN
And what about the object of my coming?

CHREMYLUS
Everything shall be according to your wish. The young man will be with you this evening.

OLD WOMAN
Oh! if you promise me his visit, I will right willingly carry the pots.

CHREMYLUS

Those are strange pots indeed! Generally the scum rises to the top of the pots, but here the pots are raised to the top of the old woman.

CHORUS

Let us withdraw without more tarrying, and follow the others, singing as we go.

Aristophanes – A Short Biography

Of Aristophanes, the greatest comedian of his age, and perhaps of all the ages, history contains few notices, and these of doubtful credit. Even the dates of his birth and death can only be inferred from his works, the former being estimated at 456 B.C. and the latter at 380. Many cities claimed the honor of giving him birth, the most probable story making him the son of Philippus of Ægina, and therefore only an adopted citizen of Athens. On this point some confusion has arisen from an attempt of Cleon to deprive Aristophanes of his civic rights, on the ground of illegitimacy, in revenge for his frequent invectives. The charge was disproved, thus pointing to the Athenian parentage of the comic poet, though as to this there is no trustworthy evidence. He was doubtless educated at Athens, and among other advantages is said to have been a disciple of Prodicus, though in his mention of that sophist he shows none of the respect due to his reputed master.

It was under the mighty genius of Aristophanes that the old Attic comedy received its fullest development. Dignified by the acquisition of a chorus of masked actors, and of scenery and machinery, and by a corresponding literary elaboration and elegance of style, comedy nevertheless remained true both to its origin and to the purposes of its introduction into the free imperial city. It borrowed much from tragedy, but it retained the Phallic abandonment of the old rural festivals, the license of word and gesture, and the audacious directness of personal invective. These characteristics are not features peculiar to Aristophanes. He was twitted by some of the older comic poets with having degenerated from the full freedom of the art through a tendency to refinement, and he took credit to himself for having superseded the time-honored can can and the stale practical joking of his predecessors by a nobler kind of mirth. But in boldness, as he likewise boasted, he had no peer; and the shafts of his wit, though dipped in wine-lees and at times feathered from very obscene fowl, flew at high game. He has been accused of seeking to degrade what he ought to have recognized as good; and it has been shown by competent critics that he is not to be taken as an impartial or accurate authority on Athenian history. But, partisan as he was, he was also a genuine patriot, and his very political sympathies—which were conservative—were such as have often stimulated the most effective political satire, because they imply an antipathy to every species of excess. Of reverence he was, however, altogether devoid; and his love for Athens was that of the most free-spoken of sons. Flexible, even in his religious notions, he was in this, as in other respects, ready to be educated by his times; and, like a true comic poet, he could be witty at the expense even of his friends, and, it might almost be said, of himself. In wealth of fancy and in beauty of lyric melody he ranks high among the great poets of all times.

It has been said that Aristophanes was an unmannerly buffoon, and so, indeed, he was, among his other faults. Nor was he at all justified in stooping to this degradation, whether it were that he was instigated by coarse inclinations, or that he held it necessary to gain over the populace, that he might have it in his power to tell such bold truths to the people. At least he makes it his boast that he did not court the laughter of the multitude so much as his rivals did, by mere indecent buffoonery, and that in this respect he brought his art to perfection. Not to be unreasonable, we should judge him from the standpoint of his own times, in respect of those peculiarities which make him offensive to us. On certain points, the ancients had quite a different morality from ours, and certainly a much freer one. This arose from their religion, which was a real worship of Nature, and had given sanctity to many public ceremonies which grossly violate decency. Moreover, as in consequence of the seclusion of their women, the men were almost always together, a certain coarseness entered into their conversation, as in such circumstances is apt to be the case.

The strongest testimony in favor of Aristophanes is that of Plato, who, in one of his epigrams, says that "the Graces chose his soul for their abode." The philosopher was a constant reader of the comedian, sending to Dionysius the elder a copy of the Clouds, from which to make himself acquainted with the Athenian republic. This was not intended merely as a description of the unbridled democratic freedom then prevailing at Athens, but as an example of the poet's thorough knowledge of the world, and of the political conditions of what was then the world's metropolis.

In his Symposium, Plato makes Aristophanes deliver a discourse on love, which the latter explains in a sensual manner, but with remarkable originality. At the end of the banquet, Aristodemus, who was one of the guests, fell asleep, "and, as the nights were long, took a good rest. When he was awakened, toward daybreak, by the crowing of cocks, the others were also asleep or had gone away, and there remained awake only Aristophanes, Agathon and Socrates, who were drinking out of a large goblet that was passed around, while Socrates was discoursing to them. Aristodemus did not hear all the discourse, for he was only half awake; but he remembered Socrates insisting to the other two that the genius of comedy was the same as that of tragedy, and that the writer of the one should also be a writer of the other. To this they were compelled to assent, being sleepy, and not quite understanding what he meant. And first Aristophanes fell asleep, and then, when the day was dawning, Agathon."

The words applied by Goethe to a shrewd adventurer, "mad, but clever," might also be used of the plays of Aristophanes, which are the very intoxication of poetry, the Bacchanalia of mirth. For mirth will maintain its rights as well as the other faculties; therefore, different nations have set apart certain holidays for jovial folly, and such as their saturnalia, their carnival, that being once satisfied to their hearts' content, they might keep themselves sober all the rest of the year, and leave free room for serious occupation. The old comedy is a general masquerade of the world, beneath which there passes much that is not allowed by the common rules of propriety; but at the same time much that is amusing, clever, and even instructive is brought to light, which would not have been possible but for the demolition for the moment of these barricades.

However corrupt and vulgar Aristophanes may have been in his personal propensities, however much he may offend decency and taste in his individual jests, yet in the plan and conduct of his poems in general, we cannot refuse him the praise of the carefulness and masterly skill of the finished artist. His language is infinitely graceful; the purest Atticism prevails in it, and he adapts it with great skill to all tones, from the most familiar dialogue to the lofty flight of the dithyrambic ode. We cannot doubt that he would have also succeeded in more serious poetry, when we see how at times he lavishes it, merely to annihilate its impression immediately afterward. This elegance is rendered the more attractive by contrast, since on the one hand he admist the rudest expressions of the people, the dialects, and even the mutilated Greek of barbarians, while on the other, the same arbitrary caprice which he brought to his views of universal nature and the human world, he also applies to language, and by composition, by allusion and personal names, or imitation of sound, forms the strangest words imaginable. His versification is not less artificial than that of the tragedians; he uses the same forms, but otherwise modified, as his personages are not to be impressive and dignified, but of a light and varied character; yet with all this seeming irregularity he observes the laws of metre no less strictly than the tragic poets do.

As we cannot help recognizing in Aristophanes' exercise of his varied and multiform art, the richest development of almost every poetical talent, so the extraordinary capacities of his hearers, which may be inferred from the structure of his works, are at every fresh perusal a matter of astonishment. Accurate acquaintance with the history and constitution of their country, with public events and proceedings, with the personal circumstances of almost all remarkable contemporaries, might be expected from the citizens of a democratic republic. But, besides this, Aristophanes required from his audience much poetic culture; especially they had to retain in their memories the tragic masterpieces, almost word by word, in order to understand his parodies.

The old comedy of the Greeks would have been impossible under any other form of government than a complete and unrestricted democracy; for it exercised a satirical censorship unsparing of public and private life, of statesmanship, of political and social usage, of education and literature, in a word, of everything which concerned the city, or could amuse the citizens. Retaining all the license, the riot and exuberance which marked its origin, it combined with this an expression of public opinion in such form that neither vice, misconduct, nor folly could venture to disregard it. If it was disfigured by grossness and licentiousness, this, it must be remembered, was in keeping with the sentiment of Dionysian festivals, just as a decorous cheerfulness was expected at festivals in honor of Apollo or Athena. To omit these features from comedy would be to deprive it of its most popular element, and without them the entertainment would have fallen flat.

Greek literature was immeasurably rich in this department: the names of the lost comedians, most of whom were very prolific, and of their works, so far as we are acquainted with them, would alone form a bulky catalogue. Although the new comedy unfolded itself, and flourished only for some eighty years, the number of plays certainly amounted to a thousand at least; but time has made such havoc with this superabundance of works that nothing remains except detached fragments in the original language, in many cases so disfigured as to be unintelligible, and in the Latin, a number of translations or adaptations of Greek originals.

For a comic poet who was unquestionably at the head of the fraternity, and in sentiment was intensely patriotic, the consciousness of his recognized power and the desire to use it for the good of his native city must ever have been the prevailing motives. At Athens such a man held an influence resembling rather that of the modern journalist than the modern dramatist; but the established type of comedy gave him an instrument such as no public satirist ever wielded, before or since. He was under no such limitations as to form or process, allusion or emphasis, as is the modern dramatist, and could indulge in the wildest flights of extravagance. After his keenest thrust or most passionate appeal, he could at once change his subject from the grave to the burlesque, and, in short, there was no limit to his field for invective and satire.

"Aristophanes," as one of his critics remarks, "is for us, the representative of old comedy." But it is important to notice that his genius, while it includes, also transcends the genius of the old comedy. He can denounce the frauds of Cleon, he can vindicate the duty of Athens to herself and to her allies with a stinging scorn and a force of patriotic indignation which make the poet almost forgotten in the citizen. He can banter Euripides with an ingenuity of light mockery which makes it seem for the time as if the leading Aristophonic trait was the art of seeing all things from their prosaic side. Yet it is neither in the denunciation nor in the mockery that he is most individual. His truest and highest faculty is revealed by those wonderful bits of lyric writing in which he soars above everything that can move laughter or tears, and makes the clear air thrill with the notes of a song as free, as musical and as wild as that of the nightingale invoked by his own chorus in the Birds. The speech of True Logic in the Clouds, the praises of country life in the Peace, the serenade in the Eccleziazusae, the songs of the Spartan and Athenian maidens in the Lysistrata, above all, perhaps the chorus in the

Frogs, the beautiful chant of the Initiated—these passages, and such as these, are the true glories of Aristophanes. They are the strains, not of an artist, but of one who warbles for pure gladness of heart in some place made bright by the presence of a god. Nothing else in Greek poetry has quite this wild sweetness of the woods. Of modern poets Shakespeare alone, perhaps, has it in combination with a like richness and fertility of fancy.

A sympathetic reader of Aristophanes can hardly fail to percieve that, while his political and intellectual tendencies are well marked, his opinions, in so far as they color his comedies, are too definite to reward, or indeed to tolerate, analysis. Aristophanes was a natural conservative. His ideal was the Athens of the Persian wars. He disapproved the policy which had made Athenian empire irksome to the allies and formidable to Greece; he detested the vulgarity and the violence of mob-rule; he clave to the old worship of the gods; he regarded the new ideas of education as a tissue of imposture and impiety. How far he was from clearness or precision of view in regard to the intellectual revolution which was going forward appears from the Clouds, in which thinkers and literary workers who had absolutely nothing in common are treated with sweeping ridicule as prophets of a common heresy. Aristophanes is one of the men for whom opinion is mainly a matter of feeling, not of reason. His imaginative susceptibility gave him a warm and loyal love for the traditional glories of Athens, however dim the past to which they belonged; a horror of what was offensive or absurd in pretension. The broad preferences and dislikes thus generated were enough not only to point the moral of comedy, but to make him, in many cases, a really useful censor for the city. The service which he could render in this way was, however, only negative. He could hardly be, in any positive sense, a political or a moral teacher for Athens. His rooted antipathy to intellectual progress, while it affords easy and wide scope for his wit, must, after all, lower his rank. The great minds are not the enemies of ideas. But as a mocker—to use the word which seems most closely to describe him on this side—he is incomparable for the union of subtlety with the riot of comic imagination. As a poet, he is immortal; and, amont Athenian poets, he has for his distinctive characteristic that he is inspired less by that Greek genius which never allows fancy to escape from the control of defining, though spiritualizing reason, than by such ethereal rapture of the unfettered fancy as lifts Shakespeare or Shelley above it,—

"Pouring out his full soul
In profuse strains of unpremeditated art."

Aristophanes – A Concise Bibliography

Surviving Plays

The Acharnians (425 BC)
The Knights (424 BC)
The Clouds (original 423 BC, uncompleted revised version from 419 BC – 416 BC survives)
The Wasps (422 BC)
Peace (first version, 421 BC)
The Birds (414 BC)
Lysistrata (411 BC)
Thesmophoriazusae or The Women Celebrating the Thesmophoria (first version c.411 BC)
The Frogs (405 BC)
Ecclesiazusae or The Assemblywomen; (c. 392 BC)
Wealth (second version, 388 BC)

Dated But Lost Plays

Banqueters (427 BC)
Babylonians (426 BC)
Farmers (424 BC)
Merchant Ships (423 BC)
Clouds (first version) (423 BC)
Proagon (422 BC)
Amphiaraus (A414 BC)
Plutus (first version, 408 BC)
Gerytades (probably 407 BC)
Cocalus (387 BC)
Aiolosicon (second version, 386 BC)

Undated Lost Plays
Aiolosicon (first version)
Anagyrus
Frying-Pan Men
Daedalus
Danaids
Centaur
Heroes
Lemnian Women
Old Age
Peace (second version)
Phoenician Women
Polyidus
Seasons
Storks
Telemessians
Triphales
Thesmophoriazusae (Women at the Thesmophoria Festival, second version)
Women in Tents